C000173400

By car to the beach – this picture, taken from the air near Pleasureland, shows a section of the 7,000 cars which crowded on to Southport's beach on Easter Monday, April, 1960.

Cover shot: magical entertainment from a Punch and Judy show on the crowded Southport beach, July, 1950.

Introduction by Geoff Wright
Content, Design & Production: Vicky Andrews
Cover Design: Rick Cooke

Pictures courtesy of the
Liverpool Post and Echo,
Geoff Wright, Southport Visiter, Mirrorpix,
With special thanks to Brian Johnston

Contact us: lostliverpool@trinitymirror.com

Advertising: Paul Ritson
Business Development Executive
0151 239 5918

Trinity Mirror Media

Managing Director: Ken Rogers
Senior Editor: Steve Hanrahan
Editor: Paul Dove
Senior Art Editor: Rick Cooke
Senior Marketing Executive: Claire Brown
Sales and Marketing Manager: Elizabeth Morgan
Sales and Marketing Assistant: Karen Cadman

Printed by Buxton Press
ISBN 9781908695468

A rollercoaster ride and day to remember at Southport in June 1967.

Introduction, by historian and journalist, Geoff Wright

The Floral Hall in the 1960s.

'COME to sunny Southport' is not a mythical yarn spun by a monicled manorial lord or a tourism supremo hiding behind floral-tinted spectacles – the resort does, and has always enjoyed, the comfort of mild winters and warm summers.

Somewhat bracing is the worst you can expect whilst strolling the Victorian pier, the wide-breadth of the Promenade, sandhills and seafront. But that is the here and now – few holidaymakers would realise that behind the solid plastic buckets and spades, golden sand castles and pier-frontaged obelisk, lays an interestingly historic past full of intrigue, disaster and determination.

It was oh so different a thousand years ago, when the site of modern-day Southport was a wild coastal tract surrounded – hemmed in like an island – by the Irish Sea, Martin Mere, River Douglas and Alt, other

The sea was very much in evidence at Southport when this scene was sketched in 1856.

watercourses and small lakes, marshland and mosses (wetlands) and of course sandy hillocks.

Where the Mersey sand and Ribble sludge met, natives of true Viking descent pursued a 'strand-looping' economy fishing, fowling, and primitive small-scale farming.

Occasional wrecking and smuggling came much later to

their rustic descendants, who profiteered from misguided traffic to Liverpool and the Isle of Man.

Timber was then scavenged to form the frame of their rude dwellings, cottages of mud and thatch – or rather wattle and daub – scattered in sandy hamlets, embossomed in the sandhills, all snug and rural. ➤

William Sutton.

➤ Absent of a nucleated setting, the isolated Church Town (Otegrimele in the Domesday Book) – with its little old church dating to the 12th century – mothered the infantile watering-hole some.

Awaiting its birth, the link was just three miles away, via the long, straight (Roman-style) vista Kirk-gata (Churchgate), then the main coastal trackway to the ancient manor house, mill, dovecote and ale-houses.

It must be remembered that even the former medieval village would not have altered at any great pace from its oldie-worldie existence if it hadn't have been for the Leeds-Liverpool Canal, with the nearest stop being around Scarisbrick.

The infant sea-side resort (formerly called South Hawes), mushroomed from a humble fisherman's hamlet (an anchorage rather than a port) and rustic agricultural backwater, to become a magnet for industrialists and merchants eager to invest in vacant rural land, to hopefully elevate themselves to a status of high dynasty in the politically naive 'open-to-offers' Lancashire outpost.

The tide turned in the late 18th century when William ('Duke') Sutton, landlord of Churchtown's Black Bull beer-house recognised potential in the barren land to attract visitors, and unbeknown to him, the future of South-Port was sealed.

Dressed in his finery – black velvet coat, pearl buttons and ruffled shirt, soft billycock hat, knee breeches and gaiters – he was the Billy Butlins of his day. Bathing in sea water was the vogue, so that is what he would cater for!

Squatting on barren land without a lease or manorial permission, Sutton and his ramshackled kiosk on the high water line, saw him transporting pleasure-seekers to his plebian summer gatherings, with ale and 'baggin' up for grabs.

On offer, for some, was a spot of what in modern-day parlance is called 'skinnydipping' in the sea, while early brazen Victorians eluded to it as undraped, health-giving 'bathing' (that is washing) in the briny waters, purely for medicinal reasons, to envigorate their frailties.

It quickly became an extremely pleasant seaside village, laying down its modest claim more than two centuries ago, by promoting the virtues of its mild air and clean waters as a healer of all that ails.

The town's motto therefore became 'Salus Populi' – 'health of the people'.

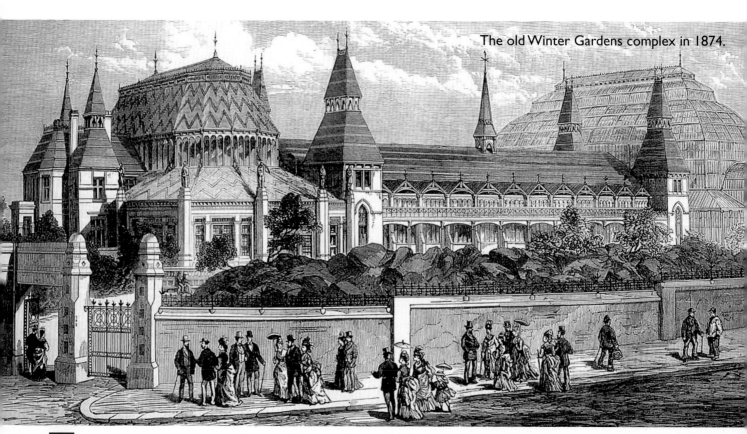

The old Winter Gardens complex in 1874.

Amidst a sahara-like sandy coastline, tucked between a barren, windswept valley, soon arose the magnificent Lord Street.

The reason for its gracious width, which is an architectural feature, is that there was a slack (filled by tidal excess) down the middle, so houses were set far back on both sides.

The preliminary planned layout of Lord Street and general building in the early district, testifies to the care and forethought of the landowners.

Victorian Southport was essentially built in an age of individualism, and is still a rich kaleidoscope of architectural styles.

Who could have imagined the place would become a fashionable centre for the well-to-do, as merchants and industrialists created opulent new villas – while fish hawkers rumbled about their business in donkey carts with fresh seafood produce to market, and weatherbeaten fisherfolk walked the streets determinedly hawking their inexpensive ware.

The coming of the railways between 1849 and 1884 really put developing Southport on the map as a top town – one of Britain's premier seaside resorts.

The Victoria Hotel and Baths were then built on the newly-

The Royal Clifton Hotel.

created promenade, while bathing machines were still sited by the shore.

Now, imagine seagulls screeching around the 1860 built 1,200-yard long iron pier (later extended to 1,400 yards to become the longest pier in the country), as 'Nobbies' sailed up the channel to unload.

The new pier, punctuating the authentic maritime atmosphere, provided moorings for a multitude of vessels, from fishing smacks to steamers, with tugs and pilot boats plying the busy channels while two and three-masted ships lay anchored, waiting for the tide or weather to turn.

Then there were excursional tales of the miniature port's pleasure paddle steamships cruising the north-west coastline (until 1922).

Things really looked up when the incredible Winter Gardens complex was created in 1874, followed by new businesses and shops and, the building of the prestigious Royal (Clifton) Hotel – which took its licence from the old defunct 'Duke's Folly'.

Man should not build his home in the sand? Well, Sutton did, then followed by others, and hey presto, Southport appeared!

From time immemorial, settlers along this isolated, god-forsaken land, plied the natural watercourses on its doorstep or created their own – as with two marine lakes – later joined to become the largest artificial lake in Britain.

However, it was the spread of the tramway network that helped knit and create the town's infrastructure, coinciding with the main period of borough development.

Guide books boasted Southport had probably a greater length ➤

W G Herdman painting of the Southport Visiter office on Lord Street, 1848.

➤ of tramway – in proportion to population – than any other town in the UK, which was quite a feat.

Lancashire's triple, separate horse-drawn tramway system, was indeed the densest tram network in Britain.

Then, from 1901, trailing sparking trolleypoles along overhead wires, the fleet of 20 electric streetcars (none of them named 'Desire') swished along under the mass of mature trees, from Churchtown's wonderful Botanic Gardens to the built-up areas of Birkdale.

With the huge sandhills long brushed away, the dominant portion of Lords' Street (as it was called originally) was paved with granite stones – other major roadways had stone setts with cubes and cobbles.

The 'main drag' appeared narrower, due to a five-foot high privet running the entire length along the kerb, on the garden (Town Hall) side. The thoroughfare certainly lacked the spaciousness which is now the main feature of this exceptionally fine boulevard.

From this preamble, recording the embryonic rise of the resort from its metamorphosis to a successfully bustling town, the end of the 19th century marked, in many ways, the end of the old and the opening of a new chapter in the rosy development of Southport.

Elegant and opulent Victorian Southport had become 'Montpelier of the North' – a 'Garden City' by the sea.

The creation and development of this salt-sprayed sleepy retreat had stemmed from industrial 'Lanky'.

The county's entrepeneurial businessmen, the import of capitalists from the heart of commercial Lancashire, helped build on what the enterprising Will Sutton had conceived.

This jolly violin-playing victualler from historic Church-Town, had inspired the rejuvenation of a medieval sea-bathing (and much drinking) festival.

Popularised for the red-rose county's working-classes, the resulting idyllic sea-side haven was planned with real purpose from the very start, through well-defined stages.

Alongside these, people of 'quality' and money developed the new town in graceful, salubrial and aristocratic fashion, a refined and genteel haven for the hard-working mill-town folk seeking somewhere softer than Blackpool.

Then – at a time when scrumptious shrimp teas and glorious sunsets were the order of the day – there were the bustled spinsters and their aspirations of residing here to dream out their retirement, and the crinolin-attired ladies in white-laced gloves and their multi-layered skirts, promenading easily along the seafront showing themselves off to the keen wealthy entrepeneurs.

It was from this backdrop that the seaside town of Southport blossomed, with classic aspirations for the future.

With its crowd-flocking attractions the town has had to try and move with the times, but retaining its unique Victorian character.

But the town has always flirted with a split-personality, confusingly not knowing what it wants to be, to the frustration of many.

From the 'good old days' Southport has lost its trams; Vulcan Motors; lifeboats; Kew and Winter Gardens; motor-racing and plane-flights on and above the beach.

Add to these its domed market and bandstand, numerous fountains and statues; and in more recent times, Birkdale's grand Palace Hotel and Ainsdale Lido; the 'Little People' Model Village; beauty pageants and Rosebuds.

ALL of its old cinemas, the Kingsway nightclub; the Botanic museum, and many other architectural delights and fine establishments, as well as Red Rum and the shrimping industry!

Gone are Peter Pan's, the ultimate escapism of old Pleasureland – along with the squeal of excited girls on the Cyclone roller-coaster, laughter (and fun-fear) of TraumaTizer riders – the open air Sea Bathing Lake and zoo have disappeared. The times they are a-changing.

However, one thing Southport has always offered is escapism, a release from the noise, grime, hustle and bustle of the large towns and cities, a family retreat for work and school weary souls – a fun place to visit and live.

For generations, daytrippers and weekend tourists have flocked here in their millions, for seaside summers at this magical weekend playground, enchanted by its diversity and all-year-round entertainment.

Modern-day Southport may have lost many of its well-loved and traditional haunts, but with its distinctive boulevard-styled Lord Street, annual Southport Flower Show and Rotten Row, the golfing paradise of Europe now has a rejuvenated King's Gardens; the popular Hesketh Park has been revamped, and the much-loved ➤

The conservatory in the Botanic Gardens.

The Botanic Gardens Museum, opened in 1876.

Peter Pan's Playground and Pool, perfect for picnics and paddling, seen here in August, 1970.

➤ Botanic Gardens will hopefully return to its former glory.

Then there is the Lakeside Miniature Railway; new Model Village; Marine Way suspension bridge; new Ramada complex; Floral Hall and Southport Theatre complex; the Little Theatre, new multiplex cinema and bowling centre all on the seafront, plus fine eating houses.

This classic resort is again on the up and up, and improving all the time!

New Pleasureland is a phoenix continually rising, to hopefully soon again rule supreme with exciting rides, penny arcades and sidestalls all consumed by the mouth-watering aroma of candy-floss and sugar-laced doughnuts; and the majestic pier still promises an energising walk out into the sea – or a trundle there on the little train.

Things are not the same – just different!

For those of you who know and love this elegant resort, this magazine will twirl you back on a white-knuckle pictorial ride to revisit that magical playground of your past, with several bucket loads of sun-drenched images recreating the atmosphere engrained in all those youthful memories.

This is a picturesque trip down memory lane, packed to reveal a sequence of magical images liberated from dimly-lit cupboards, dusty shelves and cobwebby cabinets, to re-energise a range of over 100 photographs depicting grandiose Victorian splendour right up to the noughty 1990s, through the crazy 60s which many of you may regard as the resort's golden era.

Published as part of the Liverpool ECHO and Post's best-selling heritage collection, in partnership with the Southport Visiter, this magazine will appeal to anybody interested in Southport's glorious past, and makes the perfect gift for those who love to visit, as well as proud Sandgrounders.

Enriched with surprising delights, the resort's past glories can be treasured – forever!

These charming images taken by Visiter photographers show an era when life in Southport was lived at a more sedate pace. The pier is seen from different angles, one shot capturing impeccably dressed ladies promenading along in their summer bonnets. In the late Victorian era, piers were all the rage.

Talk of a pier in Southport had been aired since the 1840s, but it wasn't until 1859 that work finally began. Engineers, pile-drivers, riveters, drillers, hole-borers and painters built a mighty pier whose metal limbs stretched 3,600ft into the Irish Sea. This was Britain's longest pleasure pier and the grand opening on August 2, 1860, was national news.

Above, a busy day on the pier – and roads – in the 1960s.
Bottom, Casino Theatre and pier entrance in 1964.

Above, a world of seaside fun awaits in the 1970s. Right, June, 1963, and this little girl wonders whether to walk or ride the pier experience.

An aerial view of the pier captured
in August 1970. A beloved jewel in
Southport's crown, the Grade II pier
achieved listed status in 1976, has
survived storm damage and fires and
been at the centre of a major campaign.
It was closed to the public in the
1990s for safety reasons, but then a
restoration programme began which
saw it reopen in 2003. The same year
it was named Pier of the Year by the
National Piers Society and continues to
draw crowds from all over the country.

Above, a winter stroll in January, 1971.
Left, hooked on fishing – members of Southport Sea Angling Club wait for a bite in May, 1961.
Below, high tide and Pleasureland viewed from the cafe, captured by Liverpool ECHO photographer Stephen Shakeshaft, in 2006.

Birds-eye view of a busy holiday
town and the Marine Lake in 1968.

Pedestrians make use of the new Venetian bridge in King's Gardens, while rowers opt for a more leisurely way to enjoy the sights, 1931. The ornamental bridge was built over Southport Marine Lake, giving direct access from the lower promenade to the bathing lake.

Jets bring new life to the Marine Lake in 1960. The previous year, it was claimed that: "Boating is finished in Southport". The lake had been losing money for years and showed no signs of ever making a profit. There were even suggestions that it might as well be filled in. But the addition of two £1,000 turbo jet speedboats saw a different story. Councillor Harold barber, chairman of the Publicity and Attractions Committee, said at the time:
"A sedate trip in a rowing boat does not suit the young man of today. He wants more excitement." Holidaymakers have been visiting the lake since the 1890s and the Boating Company was formed in August 1899.

The rowing boats on the Marine Lake were a popular attraction during the Easter weekend of 1953.

Above, dinghies silhouetted against a sparkling Marine Lake in April, 1988, as the West Lancs Yacht Club 24-Hour race comes to an end. Bottom, June, 1972, and just past the Floral Hall Gardens, a seemingly well-choreographed 'sail-by' whizzes past.

Sail away – a view from the sailing club headquarters over the Marine Lake in 1962.

Below, water skiing at Southport – with or without a boat. On the first day of summertime, in April, 1960, James Baybutt is seen in full flight on the Marine Lake, being towed by the car driven by his wife, Mildred.

The summer of 1960 and you just can't keep showgirls Lynn Paton and Vera Williamson away from the beach.

They never sang "Oh, I do like to be beside the seaside" in Southport. The vast beach could well have been called Lancashire's Sahara Desert, with the Irish Sea a watery oasis a long, long way towards the horizon. Pictured right, Southport beach and Pleasureland in April 1960. Below, a lost tradition that's still well within living memory – the Lancashire wakes weeks. During Wigan's holiday week, which apparently was 'in full swing' on July 5, 1960, these Wigan youngsters are enjoying (to differing degrees) donkey rides on Southport sands.

A warning of what happens when several thousand people simultaneously decide to get into the great outdoors to lose themselves in the empty space and sky of Southport beach. This was back in May, 1962 – and, apparently, some of the day-trippers have only just got home.

Rough and tumble – a group of boys wait for attention outside the St John's Ambulance hut at Ainsdale in 1960.

This little girl and her mum found it a hard job getting a spot to sit and sunbath. Temperatures suddenly rose to 16.2 degrees C in April, 1974, and everybody came out to make the most of it.

A heat wave in August, 1977. With all the attractions competing for the attention of holidaymakers, just sitting in a deck chair watching the world go by was always the biggest draw for adults.

Pictured right, the Ainsdale life saving team in July, 1965. Left to right, Colin Alty, Barry Burrows, Verdi Godwin, Tony Beanland, Terry Williams. Seated aboard the duck is driver Tony Venturini.

After 36 years of patrolling Southport's beaches, Chief lifeguard Verdi Godwin retired in 1989 (pictured below). Verdi, a professional football scout, helped rescue around 500 men, women, children and pets off Sefton's beaches. His most memorable rescue happened in 1983, when he saved three adults and a child after their yacht capsized. They rewarded him by handing over the yacht. Verdi and his crew gave it to the sea scouts.

The good weather brought thousands of cars to Southport in April, 1974. Car parks filled up early and the beach was so full that children wanting to build sandcastles had to find a spot between the rows of cars.

Easter crowds enjoy the sunshine in 1987.

For high-speed thrills there was Pleasureland, with its roller coasters and helter-skelters. By 1937, Charles Paige's Cyclone roller coaster was terrifying visitors while the Figure Eight railway promised a "mile-long" pleasure ride. Even couples strolling around the ornamental gardens surrounding the lake would have been only too aware of the human commotion generated by the rides and attractions of the distant Pleasureland. It was a journey to another world on the other side of the earth. Left, riding high at Southport in August, 1955. Below, life in the fast lane on the bumper cars in 1976.

The entrance to Southport's Pleasureland, July, 1934.

Southport in a riot of colour in 1968, taken from a holiday brochure of the time,

The first of the new generation rides was the Looping Star, installed in 1985. It was rapidly followed by the Traumatizer, which spun you so many ways you could hardly think. This land of thrills was the ultimate escape. Below, Chinaman's Dream in the 1930s. Left, when the sun shines on Pleasureland – aerial view from 1965.

The illuminated Whirl Around at Southport, 1971.

Pleasureland's River Caves and the Sunshine House School celebrated their 70th birthdays in 1988. The joint celebration was used to launch a charity appeal for the school.

Right, taking the plunge on the Log Flume in 1992. Children from across the region enjoyed a day out in Southport as part of national 'Kidsout' day. More than 1,000 children were taken in a convoy of 300 cars and given special concessionary tickets for the amusements at the resort.

Horsing around with squeals of
delight. Top left, the Cyclone in
1988. Top right, splashdown, on the
40ft high Waterboggan in 1986.

Clockwise: a view of Pleasureland taken from the cable car ride in 1992; hot wheels at the skate park in June 1979; the spinning disc ride at the famous Fun House in 1992; springing into action on the German-built Rocket, described as a reverse bungee jump – 1994.

Southport Opera House, July, 1928. The Opera House was built on Lord Street as an additional attraction to the main Winter Gardens complex. It opened in 1891 and was designed by Frank Matcham. In December, 1929, a fire raged through the building completely destroying it. The Garrick Theatre (above) was built on the site and opened in 1932.

The Garrick Theatre, said to be local architect George Tonge's finest design.

Right, the Scala Theatre pictured in 1960 – home of the Southport Repertory Theatre.

The Picturedrome, an early architectural gem, which opened in 1910. It is thought to have been the first purpose-built cinema in the North West. By the 1950s, cinema played such a large part in people's lives that there were 13 picture houses in Southport, with no less than nine on or near Lord Street.

Work on the Floral Hall nearing
completion in the 1930s.

The Floral Hall Gardens, pictured here in 1972, held regular afternoon
band concerts and most of the elderly audiences always appeared to
be asleep, or 'resting their eyes' as they would have said...

A hub of activity around the Floral Hall in 1972.

Entertainment of all kinds in the gardens, including a popular mother and child contest on this sunny day.

The Beatles played a total of 26 concerts in Southport between 1961 and 1963. Ringo Starr's first ever appearance with the Beatles was in the resort at the Kingsway on February 5, 1962, when he replaced regular drummer, Pete Best, who was ill.

Entrance to the Casino Theatre at Southport Pier, September, 1960. The original Pier Pavilion opened in 1902 and hosted many famous names, including Gracie Fields, George Formby, Charlie Chaplin, George Robey and Flanagan & Allen. After the original building was condemned by the council in 1970, Funland amusement arcade was built on the site.

Below, Perry Como proved a star draw when he visited Southport Theatre in April, 1975 – tickets for the concert sold out just hours after going on sale.

Taking advantage of the warm weather, three of the cast of the Victoria Theatre company go afloat to scan their scripts in July, 1966. Left to right, Sandra Griffin, Diane Langford and Patricia Fuller.

80 years on from the opening of the humble Picturehouse, and hundreds of people, in their cars on the beach watch the drive-in movie Nuns on the Run – July, 1990.

The Sea Bathing Lake was opened by the Earl of Derby on May 17, 1928. It was 330ft long and 212ft wide, and cost £70,000 to build.

The shape resembled a Roman amphitheatre, with shallow edges leading to a deeper central section.

The most elaborate construction at the bathing lake was the new café which, covered by a glazed dome roof, formed the focal point of the 230ft by 12ft covered arcade that ran around the sea-facing side of the lake. Rows of terraced seats provided comfort for more than 2,500 spectators.

The popularity of the bathing lake grew with the introduction of beauty contests and swimming galas.

Hollywood superstar Clark Gable caused quite a stir at the lake one sunny day in 1946. He stopped by unannounced, sporting his United States Army Air Force uniform, and drew in a crowd of hundreds while posing for pictures and soaking up the sunshine.

Catherine Birchall is reluctant to join her friend, Valerie Moody, for a dip in August, 1966.

The café at the Sea Bathing Lake nears completion in 1928.

The Sea Bathing Lake is still bustling with visitors, young and old, in this photograph from 1974.

Many things have come and gone in Southport during the last century, but the Lakeside Miniature Railway has a proud record of running every single year – even during two world wars.

It all began on May 27, 1911,

at 3pm when a consortium of businessmen officially opened the railway.

They were Dr Ladmore, a well-known Southport dental surgeon at the time, Mr Foulds, Mr Wright, Mr Read and the builder and

operator, Mr Griffin Vaughan Llewelyn, who originally named it 'Llewellyns Miniature Railway'.

The pleasant route soon became a popular tourist attraction for the town and the very first fares were 3d for adults and 1½d for children.

Main picture, Mr Graham Reece sends off a train load of children from Pier Station in the summer of 1939. Right, King George V, one of the original locomotives on the railway.

All aboard in the summer of 1973.

Harry Barlow took over the railway in 1934 when it became Lakeside Miniature Railway. Over the years there have been various engines, including Prince Charles, introduced in 1954.

Martin Lacey, from Southport Zoo, takes Nigel the lion for a stroll, 1965.

Above, Jill, the snow white baby llama, meets James Wilson at Southport Zoo in 1979. Below, zookeeper Paul Robinson takes no chances when he gives Horace the giant hornbill his dinner, 1984. Left, Kimberley Clark cuddles up to Judy the chimpanzee on a holiday outing to Southport Zoo, 1978.

TOWN CENTRE, LAND OF THE LITTLE PEOPLE, SOUTHPORT.

The Land of the Little People opened in 1957, and was a detailed scale model of an English town set in two acres of landscaped gardens. Every summer, thousands of youngsters and adults came to see the miniature hospital, school, castle, airport, farms, shops, thatched village, tiny model railway – and, of course, the Little People themselves. Right, Bill Rimmer repaints some of the mini models in February 1966. Below, peeking inside the houses in the 1980s.

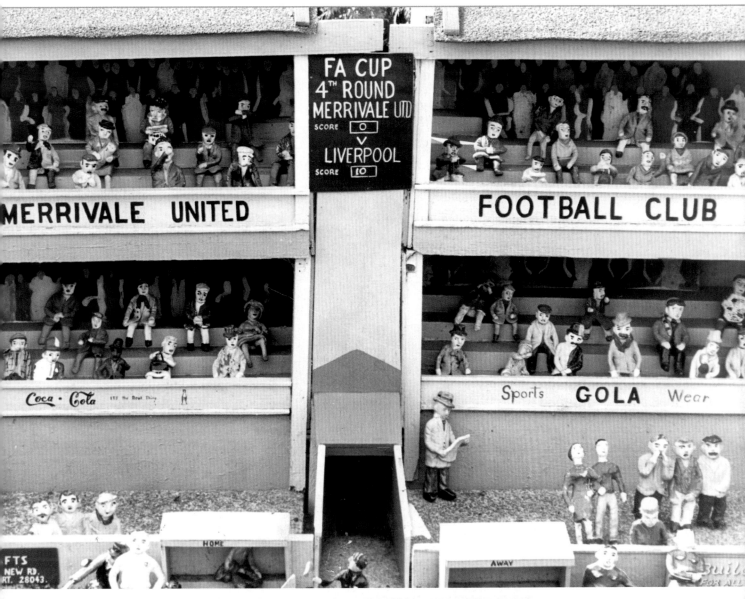

FA CUP
4TH ROUND
MERRIVALE UTD
SCORE 0
v
LIVERPOOL
SCORE 10

MERRIVALE UNITED   FOOTBALL CLUB

Coca-Cola IT'S the Real Thing   Sports GOLA Wear

HOME

FTS
NEW RD.   AWAY
RT. Z8043.

Left, a giant step for man in 1978. Above, the fantasy world of the little people – a team from the village of Merrivale play Liverpool in the Fourth Round of the FA Cup. Maybe the gigantic scoreline – Liverpool 10, Merrivale 0 – is the only claim to reality. (1979)

Over the years, the death-defying aerobatics at Southport Air Show have dazzled the enormous crowds of spectators that gather at the seafront every year.

The first Southport Air Show took place in 1991 and has grown in popularity each year. The thrilling schedule for the show includes military and civilian aircraft, the latest fast jets, vintage aircraft, helicopters, aerobatic and model aircraft displays, military manoeuvres and parachute displays. Some of the aircraft that have performed at the air show include a fly-past by the Spitfire, Hurricane fighters and the Lancaster bomber as a heroic reminder of the British aircraft that flew in the enemy skies in 1940. But the most eagerly anticipated performance of the weekend is always the Red Arrows, seen in this starburst spectacular, in 1992.

Southport Flower Show – (clockwise, from top) two trophies adorn the garden exhibited by Mr Rigg and draw the gaze of an admiring crowd in 1953; youngsters enjoy a pony ride to see the sights of the show; the smiles of these three young helpers, (left to right), Jackie Loakcart, Elizabeth Stewart and Jane Warlow, equalled the glittering of some early raindrops in 1975; an impressive display of vegetables win a gold and silver cup in 1951.

Shirley leads Daisy the cow at Southport Carnival Parade in 1991. Left, Southport Lifeboat team struggle in the tug of war competition at Southport Carnival in 1992.

'All your want-ins at Pontins' was the famous catchphrase. Sun, sea and three square meals a day... and all at a price that wouldn't break the bank. In the age of Pontins (seen here in 1973), permanently cheerful entertainers in bright blue coats were always eager to please and determined to get everyone involved in the fun. From brass band competitions to donkey derbies and It's A Knockout-style events, the Ainsdale camp had something for everyone.

Left, young and old alike enjoy afternoon tea in the sun at Southport Muncipal Gardens, taken in May, 1966. Top, Cambridge Hall, in the late 1960s, prior to its conversion to Southport Arts Centre, and in 1988. Above, postcard of the Prince of Wales Hotel – this beautiful Victorian building has long been one of the most popular hotels in the town.

The beautiful Lord Street boulevard, seen in the early 1960s in these two photographs, was the inspiration for much of Paris's architecture. Emperor Napoleon III was so enamoured by the sweeping Lord Street vista when exiled in the town that he recreated the tree-lined boulevards in Europe's most glamorous city upon his return, including the Champs-Elysees.

In 1853, a small garden was laid out in the grounds in front of Southport Town Hall. A fashionable terracotta fountain was added in 1877 and a bandstand was built in the 1890s as the latest attraction. It enjoyed its heyday from the turn of the century to the early 1900s, when band concerts drew large crowds in the day and boosted the town's popularity in the evening by playing to couples strolling around the illuminations. Dances and entertainment were staged around the Lord Street and Floral Hall Gardens bandstand. A new circular bandstand was built in 1913 but demolished in 1964 as part of Lord Street redevelopment and the creation of a new water feature garden. Architect Martin Perry designed a new one for the Eastbank Street Square Gardens, in 1984.

The 1930 Southport Corporation Military Band.

The picturesque boulevard of Lord Street in 1974.

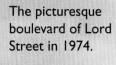

Above, a busy street scene from the 1960s. Left, the Victorian tower and frontage of former Cheshire Lines Railway Station, Lord Street, pictured in 1987. Below, the tree-lined avenues in the autumn of 1963.

Southport Football Club – November, 1965. Billy Bingham's squad resumed their Cup giant-killers role for the first time in almost 34 years, reaching the fifth round.

February 14, 1931 – McConnell of Southport FC shakes hands with Elwood of Bradford Park Avenue in the Fifth Round of the FA Cup. The final score... 1-0 to Southport.

Red Rum during a training gallop on Southport Beach in 1978.

The 1st XI of Southport and Birkdale Cricket Club take to the pitch in 1936. The club can trace its history back to 1859. Michael Braham, club history buff, muses on the origins of the sporting institution: "A letter was sent out in the Southport Visiter saying 'does anyone want to start a cricket club?'

"In the second half of the century people had to work Monday to Saturday and the introduction of the half day on Saturday meant that people had more leisure time so they started forming clubs.

"For example the rugby club in 1872, football in 1881 and Southport Golf Club, later Hesketh Golf Club in 1885."

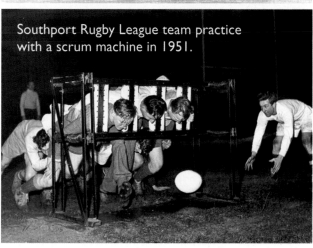

Southport Rugby League team practice with a scrum machine in 1951.

Above, Henry Cotton takes second place at the Dunlop Southport £1,600 professional golf tournament in 1934.

Left, (top to bottom) the 100-mile winners in 1932; racers get ready at the starting line; a wet sand race event in 1926; massive crowds eagerly anticipate the start of a 1929 race; a racing car at speed on Southport beach in 1930.

Ainsdale beach was once the premier venue for sand racing, due to its firm sand, and the thrill of racing attracted visitors from all over the country, not least among them Major Henry Seagraves, who famously broke the land speed record there in 1926, achieving a speed of 152 miles per hour. It was common for crowds of up to 10,000 to watch the racing until the outbreak of the Second World War saw it suspended until 1964. The hobby of racing on the dunes could be dangerous however and it was common for cars to flip over. This picture, dated 1935, is reputed to show Arthur Conan Doyle's grandson in the passenger seat of the car in the foreground as it speeds across Southport beach.

1935

These two photographs span the 39 years
between the double-deck Titan, Southport's first
Leyland bus (1929) and the Panther, seen to be
the very last word in public transport, in 1968.

Bumper to bumper on the beach during
a very busy Whit Sunday in the 1960s.

Above, a busy day at Southport during May Day in 1966. Right, it was a ten pence ticket to ride for thousands of travallers in July, 1983, at the start of the Merseyside Passenger Transport Week. Southport was besieged by daytrippers from all parts of Merseyside. As one veteran traveller said: "It was just like the good old days out..."

'Are we nearly there yet?' The final test is finding somewhere to park on this sunny day in the 1960s. Below, an Easter pilgrimage in April 1968, the golden age of seaside holidays.

LMS Jinty 7298 back on track at
Southport's Steamport in April, 1983.

Entrance to Lord Street Station viewed from the Esplanade in
May, 1951. Lord Street is immediately behind the station spire.

Top right traffic builds up on the roads outside Southport in the spring of 1961. Right, terraces of traditional red-brick guesthouses in Southport. This picture, taken in August, 1971, shows that the owners had kept up with the times by turning their front gardens into car parks.

Bank Holiday boom – cars on the
promenade during Easter Sunday in 1961.

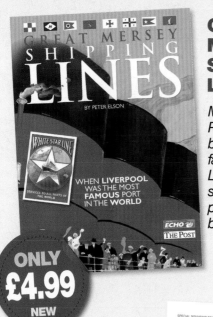

GREAT MERSEY SHIPPING LINES

Maritime expert Peter Elson looks back at at the famous Port of Liverpool at the shipping lines, the people and the buildings.

ONLY £4.99 NEW

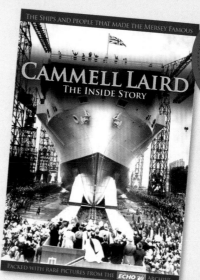

ONLY £2.00 HALF PRICE

CAMMELL LAIRD
THE INSIDE STORY

The magic and memories of the world-famous shipbuilding company, told by Harry McLeish, a proud Lairdsman of 45 years
RRP £3.99

100 YEARS OF THE TITANIC AND LIVERPOOL

This unique magazine tells the whole dramatic but tragic story of Titanic. Featuring rare and unseen images and newspaper reports from the time, it recalls how the ship believed to be unsinkable met with catastrophe on its maiden voyage.

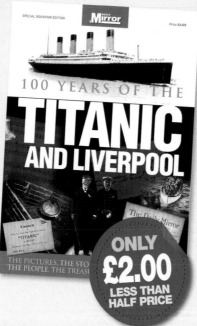

ONLY £2.00 LESS THAN HALF PRICE

QUEENS OF THE MERSEY

Commemorating the historic meeting of Cunard's Queen Elizabeth and Queen Mary 2 ocean liners to Liverpool, Queens of the Mersey looks at how Liverpool and Cunard Line have been inextricably linked for over 170 years.
RRP £3.99

ONLY £2.00 HALF PRICE

RIVER MERSEY
GATEWAY TO THE WORLD

The famous liners and passengers in Liverpool's history
RRP £4.99

ONLY £2.00 LESS THAN HALF PRICE

100 YEARS OF THE LIVER BIRDS

Born in 1911, the Liverbirds recently celebrated 100 years perched high over Liverpool looking into the city and out across the Mersey. With fantastic photographs, this is a souvenir of a century of memories.
RRP £3.99

ONLY £1.00 75% OFF

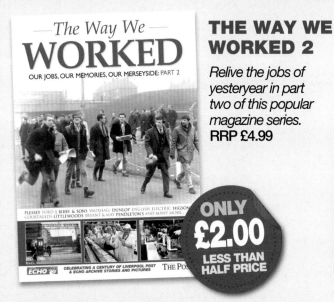

THE WAY WE WORKED 2

Relive the jobs of yesteryear in part two of this popular magazine series.
RRP £4.99

ONLY £2.00
LESS THAN HALF PRICE

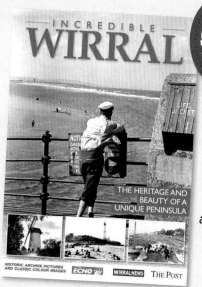

ONLY £3.00
SAVE £1.99

INCREDIBLE WIRRAL

The heritage and beauty of a unique peninsula in one glossy magazine. Historic archive pictures and classic colour images within.
RRP £4.99

LIVERPOOL THEN VOLUME 3

The third in our best-selling nostalgia series. Featuring over 100 photographs from the Liverpool Post & Echo.
RRP £4.99

ONLY £2.00
LESS THAN HALF PRICE

7 HERITAGE WONDERS OF LIVERPOOL

Seven iconic Liverpool landmarks that are known throughout the world, with stunning photographs and fascinating stories.
RRP £4.99

ONLY £3.00
SAVE £1.99

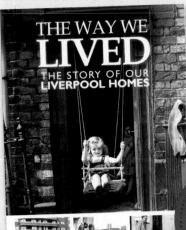

THE WAY WE LIVED

The story of our beloved homes and loving communities.
RRP £4.99

ONLY £3.00
SAVE £1.99

NEW BRIGHTON

A picture-packed tribute to the much loved seaside resort.
RRP £3.99

ONLY £2.00
HALF PRICE